Yao Ming

By Jeff Savage

AMAZING ATHLETES

Lerner Publications Company • Minneapolis

This book is available in two editions:
Library binding by Lerner Publications Company,
  a division of Lerner Publishing Group
Soft cover by First Avenue Editions,
  an imprint of Lerner Publishing Group
241 First Avenue North
Minneapolis, MN 55401 U.S.A.

Website address: www.lernerbooks.com

Library of Congress Cataloging-in-Publications Data

Savage, Jeff, 1961–
    Yao Ming / by Jeff Savage.
      p.   cm. — (Amazing athletes)
    Includes index.
    ISBN-13: 978-0-8225-2432-8 (lib. bdg. : alk. paper)
    ISBN-10: 0-8225-2432-5 (lib. bdg. : alk. paper)
    ISBN-13: 978-0-8225-2225-6 (pbk. : alk. paper)
    ISBN-10: 0-8225-2225-X (pbk. : alk. paper)
    1. Yao, Ming, 1980—Juvenile literature. 2. Basketball players—China—Biography—Juvenile literature. [1. Yao, Ming 1980– 2. Basketball players.] I. Title. II. Series.
    GV884.Y66S28 2005
    796.323'092—dc22   2003026989

Manufactured in the United States of America
2 3 4 5 6 7 – DP – 11 10 09 08 07 06

TABLE OF CONTENTS

Basketball fans around the world watched the matchup between Yao and Shaq.

PROVING HIMSELF

Yao Ming held the basketball high in the air. Shaquille O'Neal guarded him. Yao turned and shot the ball toward the basket. Swish! The Houston Rockets had the first two points of the game.

In this early season game, Yao's Rockets were playing the Los Angeles Lakers at the Compaq Center in Houston, Texas. Most people think O'Neal is the best center in the National Basketball Association (NBA). Yao was just a twenty-two-year-old **rookie** from China. He had been in the United States for only three months. But at that time Yao stood seven feet five inches tall. He was four inches taller than Shaq.

At his full height of seven feet six inches, Yao is the tallest player in the NBA.

Chinese fans cheer for Yao while watching the game on a television in Shanghai, China.

Over 10 million television viewers in the United States were watching to see how Yao would do against the great Shaq. More than 300 million people in China were tuned in too. Yao's parents

At Yao's first practice with his new Rockets teammates, he showed that he was a great passer. Passing is a special skill. "It brings teammates together," says Yao.

were watching the game in the Compaq Center stands.

Shaq tried to make a shot. Yao stepped up and **blocked** it! The Rockets had the ball. Yao took a pass inside and made a basket. The score was 4–0 in favor of Houston. Back came the Lakers. Shaq went up for his next shot, and Yao blocked it again! Wow!

Yao plays tough defense against Shaquille O'Neal of the Los Angeles Lakers.

Yao takes a shot
from the floor.

Houston took control of the ball. Yao rose up to take a fifteen-foot **jump shot.** He released the ball with a flick of the wrist. Two points! The gentle giant with the tree trunk legs was showing everyone that he was a star.

But the Lakers were defending NBA champions. They were not easy to beat. Led by O'Neal and Kobe Bryant, the Lakers stormed back to force the game into **overtime.**

With the Rockets hanging on to a two-point lead and the clock winding down, Yao set a **pick** for teammate Steve Francis. Yao rolled to the basket, took the **pass** from Francis, and **dunked**! The Rockets won the game, 108–104. Afterwards, Shaq praised the young rookie. "Yao is a great player," Shaq said. "He bumps, bangs, and dunks. He is a classy guy."

Yao and Shaq are fierce competitors, but they also respect each other.

Yao towers above his parents. He has always been tall for his age.

Growing Up Fast

Yao Ming was born September 12, 1980, in Shanghai, China. He is the only child of two tall parents. His mother, Fang Feng Di, stands six feet three inches tall. His father, Yao Zhi Yuan, is six feet seven inches. Yao's mother was captain of the Chinese national women's basketball team. His father also played basketball.

Growing up, Yao was always big for his age. At birth, he was nearly two feet long. By age nine, he stood six feet. "I was always the tallest in class," Yao remembered. "I always had to sit in the back row." At twelve years old, Yao was six feet six inches tall.

Basketball is a popular sport in China. Yao was about the same age as these boys when he started playing basketball.

More people live in China than in any other country in the world. Basketball is a popular sport in Yao's home country. More than 100 million Chinese play the game regularly. Yao began playing at age nine when he joined the Youth Sports School. Five years later, Chinese officials sent him to a special sports academy in Shanghai, where he practiced basketball for several hours each day. School officials predicted he would grow to be seven feet four inches tall. Yao lived in a room with a king-sized bed and a table and lamp. He traveled around the neighborhood on a small bicycle.

Growing up in China, Yao often watched NBA games on TV. His favorite player was Houston Rockets center Hakeem Olajuwon. Yao dreamed of someday playing in the NBA and meeting Olajuwon. Yao worked hard, and his dream came true.

In Chinese cities, many people get around town on bicycles.

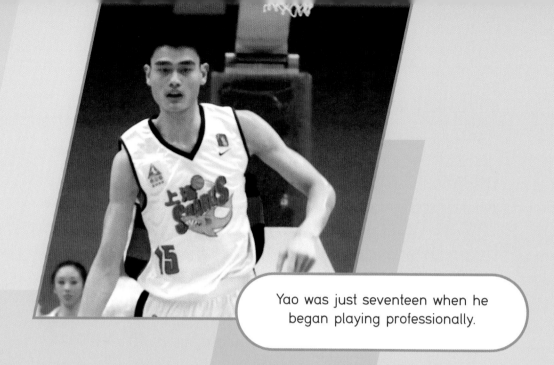

Yao was just seventeen when he began playing professionally.

COMING TO HOUSTON

By age seventeen, Yao stood seven feet tall. He could reach up and touch the basketball rim without jumping. He began playing for the Shanghai Sharks of the Chinese Basketball Association. In Yao's first season, he made about 10 points and 8 **rebounds** per game. The next season, he doubled his points to almost 21 and grabbed 13 rebounds a game.

Yao was named to the Chinese national team and was given jersey number 13. He became known as China's Little Giant. Yao's team played in the 2000 Olympic Games. Against the United States team, Yao had just 5 points and 3 rebounds before **fouling** out. The Chinese team lost, 119-72.

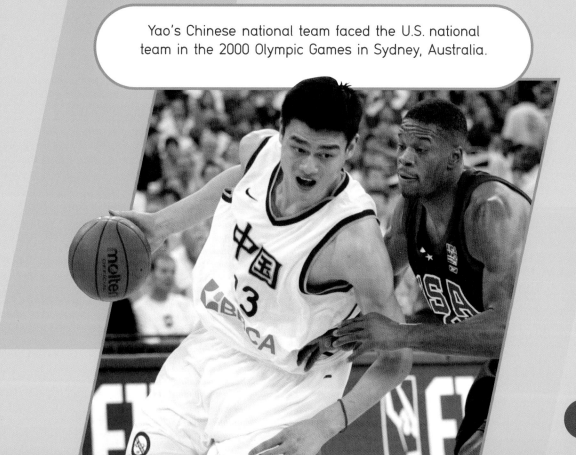

Yao's Chinese national team faced the U.S. national team in the 2000 Olympic Games in Sydney, Australia.

Yao celebrates the Sharks' victory in the CBA championship game.

Yao realized that he was not as strong as some of the U.S. players. "I need more weight training," he said. Yao began lifting weights every day. The following year, Yao played his final season for the Shanghai Sharks. He scored about 32 points and 19 rebounds per game. In the championship game, he took 21 shots and made them all! The Sharks beat the Bayi Rockets, 123–121.

Yao was China's best player. But he had dreams of playing against the world's best players in the NBA. Yao had even studied English for five years in hopes of playing in the United States. At first, the Chinese government said it would not allow Yao to play in the NBA. The Chinese government said Yao must remain in China to help the growth of Chinese basketball.

Yao plays in the United States. But he will still play for the Chinese national team in important games. Yao is very proud of his home country. He hopes to help China earn an Olympic gold medal in basketball one day.

The Houston Rockets had the first pick in the 2002 NBA **Draft.** They wanted to pick Yao. Coach Rudy Tomjanovich and other Rockets officials went to China. They talked to people in the Chinese government. Finally, Chinese officials allowed Yao to move to the United States. The Rockets took Yao with the first pick.

"Hi, Houston," said Yao. "I am coming."

Yao talks on his cell phone to the Houston Rockets' coach after he was drafted in June 2002.

REACHING HIS DREAM

Yao signed a four-year **contract** for more than $18 million. He was excited to be in the NBA. But the United States was very different from China. Yao had to get used to living in America.

Colin Pine has helped Yao adjust to his new life in the United States.

The Rockets hired a man named Colin Pine to help. Pine helped Yao understand English. Yao and his parents, along with Pine, moved into a four-bedroom house in Houston. The Rockets built Yao a special nine-foot-long bed for his bedroom and an oversized bicycle to ride around his neighborhood.

Yao became an instant superstar. The first day Yao was in Houston, Pine drove him to a store to buy some video games. A crowd of fans gathered around Yao, asking for autographs. Yao was not used to so much attention. In China, fans waved to him but kept a respectful distance.

Yao's first NBA game was shown on TV in China. More than 287 million Chinese watched the Rockets play the Indiana Pacers. But Yao played just eleven minutes. He had a bad game and finished with 2 rebounds and 0 points. Yao would need lots of practice to be a good NBA player. "I still have a lot to learn," Yao said. "It is a very long road, and it is difficult."

Yao has many fans in China as well as in the United States.

Yao has trouble hearing out of his left ear. But he does not let his handicap slow him down. Yao has to make sure he listens to people from his right ear, though.

After six games, Yao was making only about 3 rebounds and 3 points per game. The Rockets were not worried. Coach Tomjanovich told Yao to keep practicing and trying hard. Houston's fans continued to cheer for him. "They've really taken me into their hearts," said Yao.

Being a superstar was sometimes hard for Yao. Newspaper and TV reporters followed his every move. "This is the most pressure I have felt," said Yao. "Sometimes I feel like everyone is staring at me."

Still, Yao kept his sense of humor. When he was asked to name the hardest thing about living in the United States, he said it was eating cold sandwiches. He said the easiest thing was sleeping.

Meanwhile, the more Yao played, the better he got. Yao was learning to be more forceful. His coaches told him to dunk more. Players don't dunk very much in China. Some Chinese think dunking is poor sportsmanship because it makes the other player look bad. But Yao soon got used to the NBA style of play.

Basketball players in China do not usually dunk the ball. Yao has mastered this skill playing in the United States.

David Robinson takes a shot, but it is blocked by Yao.

In his tenth game in the NBA, Yao exploded for 30 points and 16 rebounds against the Dallas Mavericks. The next game, he scored 27 points against Tim Duncan and David Robinson of the San Antonio Spurs. "I haven't had many guys make me feel short," said Robinson, who is seven feet one inch tall. "Yao made me feel short and small."

Yao flies to the basket to score two points for the Houston Rockets.

SOARING LIKE A ROCKET

For the rest of 2003, Yao just kept getting better and better. He got about 13 points and 8 rebounds a game. The NBA opened an office in Beijing, the capital of China.

The league also created a website in Mandarin, or formal Chinese. Yao appeared in TV ads for coffee, computers, and sports drinks. He was one of the most popular people in China. The season ended with the Rockets barely missing the play-offs.

Yao had a great season, but he knew he needed to improve. So during the **off-season**, Yao lifted weights and got stronger. He gained

Yao is so popular that he even appears on the labels of soft drinks.

fifteen pounds of muscle. He also grew nearly another inch to seven feet six inches.

Yao's second season was even better. He made about 17.5 points and 9 rebounds a game. He completely took over some games. In one game, he grabbed 20 rebounds against the Detroit Pistons. In a game against the Atlanta Hawks, he scored 41 points and made 7 assists, his best ever. More important, he helped lead the Rockets to the play-offs for the first time in five years.

To help Yao get stronger, the Rockets encouraged him to eat more. Yao's favorite food is his mother's chicken soup. Yao has also learned to love pizza. "I'm used to Chinese things, and I love Chinese things, but I also love new experiences," he said.

Yao plays defense as Shaq makes a move to the basket.

Houston faced Shaquille O'Neal and the Los Angeles Lakers in the first round of the 2004 play-offs. Once again, Yao battled Shaq under the basket. Yao held his own against the mighty Shaq, but the Rockets lost the series, four games to one.

Off the court, Yao keeps working to improve. He tries to learn a new English word each day. Yao has a lot of pressure on him, though. "There are two billion Asian people," said Rockets owner Leslie Alexander. "And everybody is watching Yao."

China's Little Giant understands that he is representing the largest country in the world. And he knows Americans are watching too. "It seems to me I am here to do more than play basketball," said Yao. "I hope I am a good textbook."

Selected Career Highlights

2003-2004 Voted a starter in the 2004 NBA All-Star Game
Grabbed 20 rebounds in the December 6, 2003, game versus
the Detroit Pistons
Blocked 7 shots in the November 11, 2003, game versus the
Miami Heat
Scored 41 points and had 7 assists in the February 22, 2004,
game versus the Atlanta Hawks

2002-2003
Voted a starter in the 2003 NBA All-Star Game
Made about 13 points and 8 rebounds a game in his rookie
season
Named to NBA All-Rookie Team

2001-2002
Led the Shanghai Sharks to their first Chinese Basketball
Association (CBA) Championship
Scored almost 39 points with 20 rebounds and 3 blocked
shots a game in ten play-off games
Led the CBA in blocked shots for the third consecutive year
Ranked second in the CBA in both scoring and
rebounding
Received the CBA Sportsmanship Award

2000-2001 Won the Most Valuable Player award in the CBA
Third in the league in scoring, with 27.1 points per game
Led the CBA for the second straight season with 19.4 rebounds
and 5.5 blocked shots per game

1999-2000 Led the CBA in rebounds and blocked shots
Ranked sixth in the league in scoring, averaging 21.2 points

1998-1999 Ranked second in the CBA with 2.5 blocked shots per game

1997-1998 Averaged 10 points and 8.3 rebounds as a
seventeen-year-old rookie with the Sharks

Glossary

assist: a pass to a teammate that allows that teammate to score

block: stopping a shot from going in the hoop by striking the ball

contract: a written deal signed by a player and his or her team

draft: a yearly event in which teams pick new players

dunk: to put the ball forcefully through the basket

foul: illegally touching, pushing, or hitting an opponent. A player is allowed to commit a certain number of fouls before being removed from the game.

jump shot: a shot where the player jumps in the air and releases the ball

off-season: the months of the year when a team is not playing its games

overtime: extra time played to decide the winner of a game

pick: a play in which one player blocks the path of an opponent to let his teammate get past. Teams trying to score a basket use picks.

pass: to throw or bounce the basketball to a teammate in order to move the ball closer to the basket

rebound: grabbing a missed shot

rookie: a first-year player

Further Reading & Websites

Hareas, John. *Yao Ming.* New York: Scholastic, Inc., 2003.

Pyle, Linda. *Yao Ming.* Edina, MN: Abdo Publishing, 2003.

Stout, Glenn. *On the Court with . . . Yao Ming.* New York: Little, Brown and Company, 2004.

Houston Rockets Website
http://www.nba.com/rockets/
The official website of the Rockets includes team schedules, news, and information about past and present players.

Sports Illustrated for Kids
http://www.sikids.com
The *Sports Illustrated for Kids* website covers all sports, including basketball.

Yao Ming.net
http://www.yaoming.net
Yao Ming's official website provides recent news, images, statistics, game schedules, and messages from Yao to his fans.

Index

Photo Acknowledgments

Photographs are used with the permission of: © Robert Galbraith/Reuters
Newmedia Inc./CORBIS, p. 4; © Reuters NewMedia Inc/CORBIS, pp. 5, 9, 15,
18, 19; AP/Wide World Photos, pp. 6, 16, 20, 21, 23, 24; © Reuters/CORBIS, p. 7;
© Greg Fiume/NewSport/CORBIS, p. 8; © Jiang Ren/Imagine China/ZUMA
Press, pp. 10, 12, 14; © Dean Conger/CORBIS, p. 13; © Robert Seale/TSN/Icon
SMI, p. 25; © Shen Yu/Imagine China/ZUMA Press, p. 26; © Armando Arorizo/
ZUMA Press, p. 28; © Richard Carson/Reuters/CORBIS, p. 30.

Cover Image: © NewSport/CORBIS